COPYRIGHT, DISCLAIMER AND PERMISSION OF USE

Copyright, Disclaimer and Permission of Use

Copyright © 2018 by Lorena Wooten

All rights reserved. You are welcome to print a copy of this document for your personal use. Other than that, no part of this publication may be reproduced, stored, or transmitted in any form or by any means, electronic, mechanical, photocopying, recording, scanning, or other- wise, except as permitted under Section 107 or 108 of the 1976 United States Copyright Act, without the prior written permission of the author.

Requests to the author and publisher for permission should be addressed to the following email: lorenaswooten@gmail.com.

The information contained within this book is strictly for educational purposes. If you wish to apply ideas contained in this book, you are taking full responsibility for your actions. The author has made every effort to ensure the accuracy of the information within this book was correct at time of publication. The author does not assume and hereby disclaims any liability to any party for any loss, damage, or disruption caused by errors or omissions, whether such errors or omissions result from accident, negligence, or any other cause.

The methods describe within this book are the author's personal thoughts. They are not intended to be a definitive set of instructions for this project. You may discover there are other methods and materials to accomplish the same end result.

No part of this book may be reproduced or transmitted in any form or by any means, electronic or mechanical, including photocopying, recording or by any information storage and retrieval system, without written permission from the author.

THE BATTLEFIELD OF INTERCESSORS

THE BATTLEFIELD OF INTERCESSORS

THIS PRAYER JOURNAL BELONGS TO

NAME: *Ellen Cana*

THE BATTLEFIELD OF INTERCESSORS

WELCOME LETTER

Congratulations on making the greatest decision to utilize this journal as you enter into your time of Intercession. It is designed for the warriors who know their power and plan to bombard heaven on behalf of others and themselves. It is my prayer that this journal will serve as your guide to assist as you further organize your prayer life and take it to the next level. Each day, you will be presented with a new message of success and encouragement. Because I've prayed specifically about each nugget written, I am confident that when acted upon, positive results will be your portion. To reinforce what you've learned, each lesson comes complete with a fast action exercise; journal pages and powerful affirmations to accelerate your results. Within these pages you will find the inspiration you need to succeed in every area of your life.

I hope you are excited because truly, PRAYER CHANGES THINGS! The fact that you chose this book shows that you are prepared to catapult your God-breathed spirit of Intercession to another dimension. As your partner in Intercession and prayer coach, I just want to affirm that I am positioned on the wall with you and speak BY FAITH, that everything you're petitioning God for will be granted while you're in this season.

Lorena S. Wooten

PRAYER? WHY PRAY?

The purpose of prayer is to encourage consistent communication with God in order to seek His thoughts, will an plans regarding situations happening in the earth realm that impact our daily lives. Some stop at that level. However, for the Intercessor, Intercession takes us deeper into the presence God as we petition Him for others. He may share revelation or even strategic instructions during intercessory prayer. It is most important to always have a writing utensil and paper (THIS journal) nearby to scribe what the Spirit has spoken.

Intercessors are people with tremendous spiritual maturity who honor confidentiality and discretion. Intercessors must also know that they've been called by God to live a life of faith, discipline and fasting. We know that The MOST HIGH God will meet us at our level of trust, need and sacrifice.

Upon leading Intercessory prayer within your local assembly, one must be totally committed to the vision given by the set gift. Also, they must demonstrate the power of unity in order to squelch the enemy's desire to divide and conquer. Lastly, you, as God's leader in intercession, must be spiritually mature in your walk and operate in a keen level of discernment so that each utterance leaving your heart moves heaven and births the evidence of prayer in the earth. "Thy Kingdom come, Thy will be done IN EARTH as it is in Heaven..." Matthew 6:10

In this season, God is calling us into a deeper level of intercession for various spiritual infrastructures of the world. It is imperative that we go to Him on behalf of our families, churches, religious and government leaders, our local cities and states, as well as other nations. It has been proven that when all other ideologies fail, we must seek the heart and mind of God to remain in tune with what He has to say to us at every juncture.

So, let us pray.....

> IS ANYONE AMONG YOU IN TROUBLE? LET THEM PRAY. IS ANYONE HAPPY? LET THEM SING SONGS OF PRAISE.
>
> JAMES 5:13

THE BATTLEFIELD OF INTERCESSORS

MONTHLY GOALS

MY PRAYER FOCUS FOR THE MONTH:

_____

MY SPIRITUAL GOALS FOR THE MONTH:

ACTION STEPS TO ACHIEVE THESE GOALS:

_____

MY FAVORITE INSPIRATION, SCRIPTURES, AND QUOTES FOR THE MONTH:

THE BATTLEFIELD OF INTERCESSORS

MONTHLY ACTIVITIES

CHURCH & COMMUNITY ACTIVITIES

EVENT	**DATE & TIME**	**LOCATION**
_____	_____	_____
_____	_____	_____
_____	_____	_____
_____	_____	_____
_____	_____	_____
_____	_____	_____
_____	_____	_____

MY SPIRITUAL CALENDAR

SUNDAY	MONDAY	TUESDAY	WEDNESDAY	THURSDAY	FRIDAY	SATURDAY

MAY MY PRAYER BE SET BEFORE YOU LIKE INCENSE; MAY THE LIFTING UP OF MY HANDS BE LIKE THE EVENING SACRIFICE.

PSALM 141:2

THE BATTLEFIELD OF INTERCESSORS

MONTHLY GOALS

MY PRAYER FOCUS FOR THE MONTH:

_____

MY SPIRITUAL GOALS FOR THE MONTH:

ACTION STEPS TO ACHIEVE THESE GOALS:

_____

MY FAVORITE INSPIRATION, SCRIPTURES, AND QUOTES FOR THE MONTH:

THE BATTLEFIELD OF INTERCESSORS

MONTHLY ACTIVITIES

CHURCH & COMMUNITY ACTIVITIES

EVENT **DATE & TIME** **LOCATION**

_____

_____

_____

_____

_____

_____

_____

_____

MY SPIRITUAL CALENDAR

SUNDAY	MONDAY	TUESDAY	WEDNESDAY	THURSDAY	FRIDAY	SATURDAY

HE WILL RESPOND TO THE PRAYER OF THE DESTITUTE; HE WILL NOT DESPISE THEIR PLEA.

PSALM 102:7

THE BATTLEFIELD OF INTERCESSORS

MONTHLY GOALS

MY PRAYER FOCUS FOR THE MONTH:

_____

MY SPIRITUAL GOALS FOR THE MONTH:

ACTION STEPS TO ACHIEVE THESE GOALS:

_____

MY FAVORITE INSPIRATION, SCRIPTURES, AND QUOTES FOR THE MONTH:

THE BATTLEFIELD OF INTERCESSORS

MONTHLY ACTIVITIES

CHURCH & COMMUNITY ACTIVITIES

EVENT	DATE & TIME	LOCATION

MY SPIRITUAL CALENDAR

SUNDAY	MONDAY	TUESDAY	WEDNESDAY	THURSDAY	FRIDAY	SATURDAY

I CALL ON YOU, MY GOD, FOR YOU WILL ANSWER ME; TURN YOUR EAR TO ME AND HEAR MY PRAYER.

PSALM 17:6

THE BATTLEFIELD OF INTERCESSORS

MONTHLY GOALS

MY PRAYER FOCUS FOR THE MONTH:

_____

MY SPIRITUAL GOALS FOR THE MONTH:

ACTION STEPS TO ACHIEVE THESE GOALS:

_____

MY FAVORITE INSPIRATION, SCRIPTURES, AND QUOTES FOR THE MONTH:

THE BATTLEFIELD OF INTERCESSORS

MONTHLY ACTIVITIES

CHURCH & COMMUNITY ACTIVITIES

EVENT	DATE & TIME	LOCATION

MY SPIRITUAL CALENDAR

SUNDAY	MONDAY	TUESDAY	WEDNESDAY	THURSDAY	FRIDAY	SATURDAY

> "WATCH AND PRAY SO THAT YOU WILL NOT FALL INTO TEMPTATION. THE SPIRIT IS WILLING, BUT THE FLESH IS WEAK."
>
> MATTHEW 26:41

THE BATTLEFIELD OF INTERCESSORS

MONTHLY GOALS

MY PRAYER FOCUS FOR THE MONTH:

_____

MY SPIRITUAL GOALS FOR THE MONTH:

ACTION STEPS TO ACHIEVE THESE GOALS:

_____

MY FAVORITE INSPIRATION, SCRIPTURES, AND QUOTES FOR THE MONTH:

THE BATTLEFIELD OF INTERCESSORS

MONTHLY ACTIVITIES

CHURCH & COMMUNITY ACTIVITIES

EVENT　　　　　　　　**DATE & TIME**　　　　　　　**LOCATION**

_____

_____

_____

_____

_____

_____

_____

_____

MY SPIRITUAL CALENDAR

SUNDAY	MONDAY	TUESDAY	WEDNESDAY	THURSDAY	FRIDAY	SATURDAY

> **THEN YOU WILL CALL ON ME AND COME AND PRAY TO ME, AND I WILL LISTEN TO YOU.**
>
> JEREMIAH 29:12

THE BATTLEFIELD OF INTERCESSORS

MONTHLY GOALS

MY PRAYER FOCUS FOR THE MONTH:

_____

MY SPIRITUAL GOALS FOR THE MONTH:

ACTION STEPS TO ACHIEVE THESE GOALS:

_____

MY FAVORITE INSPIRATION, SCRIPTURES, AND QUOTES FOR THE MONTH:

THE BATTLEFIELD OF INTERCESSORS

MONTHLY ACTIVITIES

CHURCH & COMMUNITY ACTIVITIES

EVENT **DATE & TIME** **LOCATION**

MY SPIRITUAL CALENDAR

SUNDAY	MONDAY	TUESDAY	WEDNESDAY	THURSDAY	FRIDAY	SATURDAY

> THEREFORE I TELL YOU, WHATEVER YOU ASK FOR IN PRAYER, BELIEVE THAT YOU HAVE RECEIVED IT, AND IT WILL BE YOURS.
>
> MARK 11:24

PRAYER REQUESTS

NAME:
PRAYER REQUEST:
DATE REQUESTED:
DATE ANSWERED:

PRAYER FOCUS SCRIPTURE

NAME:
PRAYER REQUEST:
DATE REQUESTED:
DATE ANSWERED:

PRAYER FOCUS SCRIPTURE

NAME:
PRAYER REQUEST:
DATE REQUESTED:
DATE ANSWERED:

PRAYER FOCUS SCRIPTURE

NAME:
PRAYER REQUEST:
DATE REQUESTED:
DATE ANSWERED:

PRAYER FOCUS SCRIPTURE

NAME:
PRAYER REQUEST:
DATE REQUESTED:
DATE ANSWERED:

PRAYER FOCUS SCRIPTURE

PRAYER REQUESTS

NAME:
PRAYER REQUEST:
DATE REQUESTED:
DATE ANSWERED:

PRAYER FOCUS SCRIPTURE

NAME:
PRAYER REQUEST:
DATE REQUESTED:
DATE ANSWERED:

PRAYER FOCUS SCRIPTURE

NAME:
PRAYER REQUEST:
DATE REQUESTED:
DATE ANSWERED:

PRAYER FOCUS SCRIPTURE

NAME:
PRAYER REQUEST:
DATE REQUESTED:
DATE ANSWERED:

PRAYER FOCUS SCRIPTURE

NAME:
PRAYER REQUEST:
DATE REQUESTED:
DATE ANSWERED:

PRAYER FOCUS SCRIPTURE

PRAYER REQUESTS

NAME:
PRAYER REQUEST:
DATE REQUESTED:
DATE ANSWERED:

PRAYER FOCUS SCRIPTURE

NAME:
PRAYER REQUEST:
DATE REQUESTED:
DATE ANSWERED:

PRAYER FOCUS SCRIPTURE

NAME:
PRAYER REQUEST:
DATE REQUESTED:
DATE ANSWERED:

PRAYER FOCUS SCRIPTURE

NAME:
PRAYER REQUEST:
DATE REQUESTED:
DATE ANSWERED:

PRAYER FOCUS SCRIPTURE

NAME:
PRAYER REQUEST:
DATE REQUESTED:
DATE ANSWERED:

PRAYER FOCUS SCRIPTURE

PRAYER REQUESTS

NAME:
PRAYER REQUEST:
DATE REQUESTED:
DATE ANSWERED:

PRAYER FOCUS SCRIPTURE

NAME:
PRAYER REQUEST:
DATE REQUESTED:
DATE ANSWERED:

PRAYER FOCUS SCRIPTURE

NAME:
PRAYER REQUEST:
DATE REQUESTED:
DATE ANSWERED:

PRAYER FOCUS SCRIPTURE

NAME:
PRAYER REQUEST:
DATE REQUESTED:
DATE ANSWERED:

PRAYER FOCUS SCRIPTURE

NAME:
PRAYER REQUEST:
DATE REQUESTED:
DATE ANSWERED:

PRAYER FOCUS SCRIPTURE

PRAYER REQUESTS

NAME:
PRAYER REQUEST:
DATE REQUESTED:
DATE ANSWERED:

PRAYER FOCUS SCRIPTURE

NAME:
PRAYER REQUEST:
DATE REQUESTED:
DATE ANSWERED:

PRAYER FOCUS SCRIPTURE

NAME:
PRAYER REQUEST:
DATE REQUESTED:
DATE ANSWERED:

PRAYER FOCUS SCRIPTURE

NAME:
PRAYER REQUEST:
DATE REQUESTED:
DATE ANSWERED:

PRAYER FOCUS SCRIPTURE

NAME:
PRAYER REQUEST:
DATE REQUESTED:
DATE ANSWERED:

PRAYER FOCUS SCRIPTURE

PRAYER REQUESTS

NAME:
PRAYER REQUEST:
DATE REQUESTED:
DATE ANSWERED:

PRAYER FOCUS SCRIPTURE

NAME:
PRAYER REQUEST:
DATE REQUESTED:
DATE ANSWERED:

PRAYER FOCUS SCRIPTURE

NAME:
PRAYER REQUEST:
DATE REQUESTED:
DATE ANSWERED:

PRAYER FOCUS SCRIPTURE

NAME:
PRAYER REQUEST:
DATE REQUESTED:
DATE ANSWERED:

PRAYER FOCUS SCRIPTURE

NAME:
PRAYER REQUEST:
DATE REQUESTED:
DATE ANSWERED:

PRAYER FOCUS SCRIPTURE

PRAYER REQUESTS

NAME:
PRAYER REQUEST:
DATE REQUESTED:
DATE ANSWERED:

PRAYER FOCUS SCRIPTURE

NAME:
PRAYER REQUEST:
DATE REQUESTED:
DATE ANSWERED:

PRAYER FOCUS SCRIPTURE

NAME:
PRAYER REQUEST:
DATE REQUESTED:
DATE ANSWERED:

PRAYER FOCUS SCRIPTURE

NAME:
PRAYER REQUEST:
DATE REQUESTED:
DATE ANSWERED:

PRAYER FOCUS SCRIPTURE

NAME:
PRAYER REQUEST:
DATE REQUESTED:
DATE ANSWERED:

PRAYER FOCUS SCRIPTURE

PRAYER REQUESTS

NAME:
PRAYER REQUEST:
DATE REQUESTED:
DATE ANSWERED:

PRAYER FOCUS SCRIPTURE

___

NAME:
PRAYER REQUEST:
DATE REQUESTED:
DATE ANSWERED:

PRAYER FOCUS SCRIPTURE

___

NAME:
PRAYER REQUEST:
DATE REQUESTED:
DATE ANSWERED:

PRAYER FOCUS SCRIPTURE

___

NAME:
PRAYER REQUEST:
DATE REQUESTED:
DATE ANSWERED:

PRAYER FOCUS SCRIPTURE

___

NAME:
PRAYER REQUEST:
DATE REQUESTED:
DATE ANSWERED:

PRAYER FOCUS SCRIPTURE

PRAYER REQUESTS

NAME:
PRAYER REQUEST:
DATE REQUESTED:
DATE ANSWERED:

PRAYER FOCUS SCRIPTURE

NAME:
PRAYER REQUEST:
DATE REQUESTED:
DATE ANSWERED:

PRAYER FOCUS SCRIPTURE

NAME:
PRAYER REQUEST:
DATE REQUESTED:
DATE ANSWERED:

PRAYER FOCUS SCRIPTURE

NAME:
PRAYER REQUEST:
DATE REQUESTED:
DATE ANSWERED:

PRAYER FOCUS SCRIPTURE

NAME:
PRAYER REQUEST:
DATE REQUESTED:
DATE ANSWERED:

PRAYER FOCUS SCRIPTURE

PRAYER REQUESTS

NAME:
PRAYER REQUEST:
DATE REQUESTED:
DATE ANSWERED:

PRAYER FOCUS SCRIPTURE

NAME:
PRAYER REQUEST:
DATE REQUESTED:
DATE ANSWERED:

PRAYER FOCUS SCRIPTURE

NAME:
PRAYER REQUEST:
DATE REQUESTED:
DATE ANSWERED:

PRAYER FOCUS SCRIPTURE

NAME:
PRAYER REQUEST:
DATE REQUESTED:
DATE ANSWERED:

PRAYER FOCUS SCRIPTURE

NAME:
PRAYER REQUEST:
DATE REQUESTED:
DATE ANSWERED:

PRAYER FOCUS SCRIPTURE

> **BUT I TELL YOU, LOVE YOUR ENEMIES AND PRAY FOR THOSE WHO PERSECUTE YOU.**
>
> MATTHEW 5:44

> AND WHEN YOU PRAY, DO NOT KEEP ON BABBLING LIKE PAGANS, FOR THEY THINK THEY WILL BE HEARD BECAUSE OF THEIR MANY WORDS.
>
> MATTHEW 6:7

MY PRAYER TIME

DATE:_____   TIME:_____

BIBLE PASSAGES & SCRIPTURES: _____
_____

WHAT GOD IS SAYING: _____
_____

WHAT I'M THANKFUL FOR: _____
_____

JOURNAL AREA

DATE:_____   TIME:_____

_____
_____
_____
_____
_____
_____
_____

MY PRAYER TIME

DATE:_____ TIME:_____

BIBLE PASSAGES & SCRIPTURES: _____

_____

WHAT GOD IS SAYING: _____

_____

WHAT I'M THANKFUL FOR: _____

_____

JOURNAL AREA

DATE:_____ TIME:_____

_____

_____

_____

_____

_____

_____

_____

MY PRAYER TIME

DATE:_____ TIME:_____

BIBLE PASSAGES & SCRIPTURES: _____
_____

WHAT GOD IS SAYING: _____
_____

WHAT I'M THANKFUL FOR: _____
_____

JOURNAL AREA

DATE:_____ TIME:_____

_____
_____
_____
_____
_____
_____
_____

MY PRAYER TIME

DATE:_____ TIME:_____

BIBLE PASSAGES & SCRIPTURES: _____
_____

WHAT GOD IS SAYING: _____
_____

WHAT I'M THANKFUL FOR: _____
_____

JOURNAL AREA

DATE:_____ TIME:_____

_____
_____
_____
_____
_____
_____
_____

MY PRAYER TIME

DATE:_____ TIME:_____

BIBLE PASSAGES & SCRIPTURES: _____
_____

WHAT GOD IS SAYING: _____
_____

WHAT I'M THANKFUL FOR: _____
_____

JOURNAL AREA

DATE:_____ TIME:_____

_____
_____
_____
_____
_____
_____
_____

MY PRAYER TIME

DATE:_____ TIME:_____

BIBLE PASSAGES & SCRIPTURES: _____
_____

WHAT GOD IS SAYING: _____
_____

WHAT I'M THANKFUL FOR: _____
_____

JOURNAL AREA

DATE:_____ TIME:_____

_____
_____
_____
_____
_____
_____
_____

MY PRAYER TIME

DATE:_____ TIME:_____

BIBLE PASSAGES & SCRIPTURES: _____
_____

WHAT GOD IS SAYING: _____
_____

WHAT I'M THANKFUL FOR: _____
_____

JOURNAL AREA

DATE:_____ TIME:_____

_____
_____
_____
_____
_____
_____
_____

MY PRAYER TIME

DATE:_____ TIME:_____

BIBLE PASSAGES & SCRIPTURES: _____
_____

WHAT GOD IS SAYING: _____
_____

WHAT I'M THANKFUL FOR: _____
_____

JOURNAL AREA

DATE:_____ TIME:_____

_____
_____
_____
_____
_____
_____
_____

MY PRAYER TIME

DATE:_____ TIME:_____

BIBLE PASSAGES & SCRIPTURES: _____
_____

WHAT GOD IS SAYING: _____
_____

WHAT I'M THANKFUL FOR: _____
_____

JOURNAL AREA

DATE:_____ TIME:_____

_____
_____
_____
_____
_____
_____
_____

MY PRAYER TIME

DATE:_____ TIME:_____

BIBLE PASSAGES & SCRIPTURES: _____
_____

WHAT GOD IS SAYING: _____
_____

WHAT I'M THANKFUL FOR: _____
_____

JOURNAL AREA

DATE:_____ TIME:_____

_____
_____
_____
_____
_____
_____
_____

MY PRAYER TIME

DATE:_____ TIME:_____

BIBLE PASSAGES & SCRIPTURES: _____
_____

WHAT GOD IS SAYING: _____
_____

WHAT I'M THANKFUL FOR: _____
_____

JOURNAL AREA

DATE:_____ TIME:_____

_____
_____
_____
_____
_____
_____
_____

MY PRAYER TIME

DATE:_____ TIME:_____

BIBLE PASSAGES & SCRIPTURES: _____
_____

WHAT GOD IS SAYING: _____
_____

WHAT I'M THANKFUL FOR: _____
_____

JOURNAL AREA

DATE:_____ TIME:_____

_____
_____
_____
_____
_____
_____
_____

MY PRAYER TIME

DATE:_____   TIME:_____

BIBLE PASSAGES & SCRIPTURES: _____
_____

WHAT GOD IS SAYING: _____
_____

WHAT I'M THANKFUL FOR: _____
_____

JOURNAL AREA

DATE:_____   TIME:_____

_____
_____
_____
_____
_____
_____
_____

MY PRAYER TIME

DATE:_____ TIME:_____

BIBLE PASSAGES & SCRIPTURES: _____
_____

WHAT GOD IS SAYING: _____
_____

WHAT I'M THANKFUL FOR: _____
_____

JOURNAL AREA

DATE:_____ TIME:_____

_____
_____
_____
_____
_____
_____
_____
_____

MY PRAYER TIME

DATE:_____ TIME:_____

BIBLE PASSAGES & SCRIPTURES: _____
_____

WHAT GOD IS SAYING: _____
_____

WHAT I'M THANKFUL FOR: _____
_____

JOURNAL AREA

DATE:_____ TIME:_____

_____
_____
_____
_____
_____
_____
_____

MY PRAYER TIME

DATE:_____ TIME:_____

BIBLE PASSAGES & SCRIPTURES: _____
_____

WHAT GOD IS SAYING: _____
_____

WHAT I'M THANKFUL FOR: _____
_____

JOURNAL AREA

DATE:_____ TIME:_____

_____
_____
_____
_____
_____
_____
_____
_____

MY PRAYER TIME

DATE:_____ TIME:_____

BIBLE PASSAGES & SCRIPTURES: _____
_____

WHAT GOD IS SAYING: _____
_____

WHAT I'M THANKFUL FOR: _____
_____

JOURNAL AREA

DATE:_____ TIME:_____

_____
_____
_____
_____
_____
_____
_____

MY PRAYER TIME

DATE:_____ TIME:_____

BIBLE PASSAGES & SCRIPTURES: _____
_____

WHAT GOD IS SAYING: _____
_____

WHAT I'M THANKFUL FOR: _____
_____

JOURNAL AREA

DATE:_____ TIME:_____

_____
_____
_____
_____
_____
_____
_____
_____

MY PRAYER TIME

DATE:_____ TIME:_____

BIBLE PASSAGES & SCRIPTURES: _____
_____

WHAT GOD IS SAYING: _____
_____

WHAT I'M THANKFUL FOR: _____
_____

JOURNAL AREA

DATE:_____ TIME:_____

_____
_____
_____
_____
_____
_____
_____

MY PRAYER TIME

DATE:_____ TIME:_____

BIBLE PASSAGES & SCRIPTURES: _____
_____

WHAT GOD IS SAYING: _____
_____

WHAT I'M THANKFUL FOR: _____
_____

JOURNAL AREA

DATE:_____ TIME:_____

_____
_____
_____
_____
_____
_____
_____

MY PRAYER TIME

DATE:_____ TIME:_____

BIBLE PASSAGES & SCRIPTURES: _____
_____

WHAT GOD IS SAYING: _____
_____

WHAT I'M THANKFUL FOR: _____
_____

JOURNAL AREA

DATE:_____ TIME:_____

_____
_____
_____
_____
_____
_____
_____

MY PRAYER TIME

DATE:_____ TIME:_____

BIBLE PASSAGES & SCRIPTURES: _____
_____

WHAT GOD IS SAYING: _____
_____

WHAT I'M THANKFUL FOR: _____
_____

JOURNAL AREA

DATE:_____ TIME:_____

_____
_____
_____
_____
_____
_____
_____
_____

MY PRAYER TIME

DATE:_____ TIME:_____

BIBLE PASSAGES & SCRIPTURES: _____
_____

WHAT GOD IS SAYING: _____
_____

WHAT I'M THANKFUL FOR: _____
_____

JOURNAL AREA

DATE:_____ TIME:_____

_____
_____
_____
_____
_____
_____
_____

MY PRAYER TIME

DATE:_____ TIME:_____

BIBLE PASSAGES & SCRIPTURES: _____
_____

WHAT GOD IS SAYING: _____
_____

WHAT I'M THANKFUL FOR: _____
_____

JOURNAL AREA

DATE:_____ TIME:_____

_____
_____
_____
_____
_____
_____
_____

MY PRAYER TIME

DATE:_____ TIME:_____

BIBLE PASSAGES & SCRIPTURES: _____
_____

WHAT GOD IS SAYING: _____
_____

WHAT I'M THANKFUL FOR: _____
_____

JOURNAL AREA

DATE:_____ TIME:_____

_____
_____
_____
_____
_____
_____
_____

MY PRAYER TIME

DATE:_____ TIME:_____

BIBLE PASSAGES & SCRIPTURES: _____
_____

WHAT GOD IS SAYING: _____
_____

WHAT I'M THANKFUL FOR: _____
_____

JOURNAL AREA

DATE:_____ TIME:_____

_____
_____
_____
_____
_____
_____
_____

MY PRAYER TIME

DATE:_____ TIME:_____

BIBLE PASSAGES & SCRIPTURES: _____

_____

WHAT GOD IS SAYING: _____

_____

WHAT I'M THANKFUL FOR: _____

_____

JOURNAL AREA

DATE:_____ TIME:_____

_____

_____

_____

_____

_____

_____

_____

MY PRAYER TIME

DATE:_____ TIME:_____

BIBLE PASSAGES & SCRIPTURES: _____
_____

WHAT GOD IS SAYING: _____
_____

WHAT I'M THANKFUL FOR: _____
_____

JOURNAL AREA

DATE:_____ TIME:_____

_____
_____
_____
_____
_____
_____
_____

MY PRAYER TIME

DATE:_____ TIME:_____

BIBLE PASSAGES & SCRIPTURES: _____
_____

WHAT GOD IS SAYING: _____
_____

WHAT I'M THANKFUL FOR: _____
_____

JOURNAL AREA

DATE:_____ TIME:_____

_____
_____
_____
_____
_____
_____
_____

MY PRAYER TIME

DATE:_____ TIME:_____

BIBLE PASSAGES & SCRIPTURES: _____

_____

WHAT GOD IS SAYING: _____

_____

WHAT I'M THANKFUL FOR: _____

_____

JOURNAL AREA

DATE:_____ TIME:_____

_____

_____

_____

_____

_____

_____

_____

MY PRAYER TIME

DATE:_____ TIME:_____

BIBLE PASSAGES & SCRIPTURES: _____
_____

WHAT GOD IS SAYING: _____
_____

WHAT I'M THANKFUL FOR: _____
_____

JOURNAL AREA

DATE:_____ TIME:_____

_____
_____
_____
_____
_____
_____
_____

MY PRAYER TIME

DATE:_____ TIME:_____

BIBLE PASSAGES & SCRIPTURES: _____
_____

WHAT GOD IS SAYING: _____
_____

WHAT I'M THANKFUL FOR: _____
_____

JOURNAL AREA

DATE:_____ TIME:_____

_____
_____
_____
_____
_____
_____
_____

MY PRAYER TIME

DATE:_____ TIME:_____

BIBLE PASSAGES & SCRIPTURES: _____
_____

WHAT GOD IS SAYING: _____
_____

WHAT I'M THANKFUL FOR: _____
_____

JOURNAL AREA

DATE:_____ TIME:_____

_____
_____
_____
_____
_____
_____
_____

MY PRAYER TIME

DATE:_____ TIME:_____

BIBLE PASSAGES & SCRIPTURES: _____
_____

WHAT GOD IS SAYING: _____
_____

WHAT I'M THANKFUL FOR: _____
_____

JOURNAL AREA

DATE:_____ TIME:_____

_____
_____
_____
_____
_____
_____
_____

MY PRAYER TIME

DATE:_____ TIME:_____

BIBLE PASSAGES & SCRIPTURES: _____
_____

WHAT GOD IS SAYING: _____
_____

WHAT I'M THANKFUL FOR: _____
_____

JOURNAL AREA

DATE:_____ TIME:_____

_____
_____
_____
_____
_____
_____
_____
_____

MY PRAYER TIME

DATE:_____ TIME:_____

BIBLE PASSAGES & SCRIPTURES: _____
_____

WHAT GOD IS SAYING: _____
_____

WHAT I'M THANKFUL FOR: _____
_____

JOURNAL AREA

DATE:_____ TIME:_____

_____
_____
_____
_____
_____
_____
_____
_____

MY PRAYER TIME

DATE:_____ TIME:_____

BIBLE PASSAGES & SCRIPTURES: _____
_____

WHAT GOD IS SAYING: _____
_____

WHAT I'M THANKFUL FOR: _____
_____

JOURNAL AREA

DATE:_____ TIME:_____

_____
_____
_____
_____
_____
_____
_____

MY PRAYER TIME

DATE:_____ TIME:_____

BIBLE PASSAGES & SCRIPTURES: _____
_____

WHAT GOD IS SAYING: _____
_____

WHAT I'M THANKFUL FOR: _____
_____

JOURNAL AREA

DATE:_____ TIME:_____

_____
_____
_____
_____
_____
_____
_____
_____

MY PRAYER TIME

DATE:_____ TIME:_____

BIBLE PASSAGES & SCRIPTURES: _____
_____

WHAT GOD IS SAYING: _____
_____

WHAT I'M THANKFUL FOR: _____
_____

JOURNAL AREA

DATE:_____ TIME:_____

_____
_____
_____
_____
_____
_____
_____

MY PRAYER TIME

DATE:_____ TIME:_____

BIBLE PASSAGES & SCRIPTURES: _____
_____

WHAT GOD IS SAYING: _____
_____

WHAT I'M THANKFUL FOR: _____
_____

JOURNAL AREA

DATE:_____ TIME:_____

_____
_____
_____
_____
_____
_____
_____

MY PRAYER TIME

DATE:_____ TIME:_____

BIBLE PASSAGES & SCRIPTURES: _____
_____

WHAT GOD IS SAYING: _____
_____

WHAT I'M THANKFUL FOR: _____
_____

JOURNAL AREA

DATE:_____ TIME:_____

_____
_____
_____
_____
_____
_____
_____

MY PRAYER TIME

DATE:_____ TIME:_____

BIBLE PASSAGES & SCRIPTURES: _____
_____

WHAT GOD IS SAYING: _____
_____

WHAT I'M THANKFUL FOR: _____
_____

JOURNAL AREA

DATE:_____ TIME:_____

_____
_____
_____
_____
_____
_____
_____

MY PRAYER TIME

DATE:_____ TIME:_____

BIBLE PASSAGES & SCRIPTURES: _____
_____

WHAT GOD IS SAYING: _____
_____

WHAT I'M THANKFUL FOR: _____
_____

JOURNAL AREA

DATE:_____ TIME:_____

_____
_____
_____
_____
_____
_____
_____

MY PRAYER TIME

DATE:_____ TIME:_____

BIBLE PASSAGES & SCRIPTURES: _____
_____

WHAT GOD IS SAYING: _____
_____

WHAT I'M THANKFUL FOR: _____
_____

JOURNAL AREA

DATE:_____ TIME:_____

_____
_____
_____
_____
_____
_____
_____

MY PRAYER TIME

DATE:_____ TIME:_____

BIBLE PASSAGES & SCRIPTURES: _____
_____

WHAT GOD IS SAYING: _____
_____

WHAT I'M THANKFUL FOR: _____
_____

JOURNAL AREA

DATE:_____ TIME:_____

_____
_____
_____
_____
_____
_____
_____

MY PRAYER TIME

DATE:_____ TIME:_____

BIBLE PASSAGES & SCRIPTURES: _____
_____

WHAT GOD IS SAYING: _____
_____

WHAT I'M THANKFUL FOR: _____
_____

JOURNAL AREA

DATE:_____ TIME:_____

_____
_____
_____
_____
_____
_____
_____

MY PRAYER TIME

DATE:_____ TIME:_____

BIBLE PASSAGES & SCRIPTURES: _____
_____

WHAT GOD IS SAYING: _____
_____

WHAT I'M THANKFUL FOR: _____
_____

JOURNAL AREA

DATE:_____ TIME:_____

_____
_____
_____
_____
_____
_____
_____

MY PRAYER TIME

DATE:_____ TIME:_____

BIBLE PASSAGES & SCRIPTURES: _____
_____

WHAT GOD IS SAYING: _____
_____

WHAT I'M THANKFUL FOR: _____
_____

JOURNAL AREA

DATE:_____ TIME:_____

_____
_____
_____
_____
_____
_____
_____

MY PRAYER TIME

DATE:_____ TIME:_____

BIBLE PASSAGES & SCRIPTURES: _____
_____

WHAT GOD IS SAYING: _____
_____

WHAT I'M THANKFUL FOR: _____
_____

JOURNAL AREA

DATE:_____ TIME:_____

_____
_____
_____
_____
_____
_____
_____

MY PRAYER TIME

DATE:_____ TIME:_____

BIBLE PASSAGES & SCRIPTURES: _____
_____

WHAT GOD IS SAYING: _____
_____

WHAT I'M THANKFUL FOR: _____
_____

JOURNAL AREA

DATE:_____ TIME:_____

_____
_____
_____
_____
_____
_____
_____

MY PRAYER TIME

DATE:_____ TIME:_____

BIBLE PASSAGES & SCRIPTURES: _____
_____

WHAT GOD IS SAYING: _____
_____

WHAT I'M THANKFUL FOR: _____
_____

JOURNAL AREA

DATE:_____ TIME:_____

_____
_____
_____
_____
_____
_____
_____

MY PRAYER TIME

DATE:_____ TIME:_____

BIBLE PASSAGES & SCRIPTURES: _____
_____

WHAT GOD IS SAYING: _____
_____

WHAT I'M THANKFUL FOR: _____
_____

JOURNAL AREA

DATE:_____ TIME:_____

_____
_____
_____
_____
_____
_____
_____

MY PRAYER TIME

DATE:_____ TIME:_____

BIBLE PASSAGES & SCRIPTURES: _____

_____

WHAT GOD IS SAYING: _____

_____

WHAT I'M THANKFUL FOR: _____

_____

JOURNAL AREA

DATE:_____ TIME:_____

_____

_____

_____

_____

_____

_____

_____

MY PRAYER TIME

DATE:_____ TIME:_____

BIBLE PASSAGES & SCRIPTURES: _____
_____

WHAT GOD IS SAYING: _____
_____

WHAT I'M THANKFUL FOR: _____
_____

JOURNAL AREA

DATE:_____ TIME:_____

_____
_____
_____
_____
_____
_____
_____

MY PRAYER TIME

DATE:_____ TIME:_____

BIBLE PASSAGES & SCRIPTURES: _____
_____

WHAT GOD IS SAYING: _____
_____

WHAT I'M THANKFUL FOR: _____
_____

JOURNAL AREA

DATE:_____ TIME:_____

_____
_____
_____
_____
_____
_____

MY PRAYER TIME

DATE:_____ TIME:_____

BIBLE PASSAGES & SCRIPTURES: _____
_____

WHAT GOD IS SAYING: _____
_____

WHAT I'M THANKFUL FOR: _____
_____

JOURNAL AREA

DATE:_____ TIME:_____

_____
_____
_____
_____
_____
_____
_____
_____

MY PRAYER TIME

DATE:_____ TIME:_____

BIBLE PASSAGES & SCRIPTURES: _____
_____

WHAT GOD IS SAYING: _____
_____

WHAT I'M THANKFUL FOR: _____
_____

JOURNAL AREA

DATE:_____ TIME:_____

_____
_____
_____
_____
_____
_____
_____

MY PRAYER TIME

DATE:_____ TIME:_____

BIBLE PASSAGES & SCRIPTURES: _____
_____

WHAT GOD IS SAYING: _____
_____

WHAT I'M THANKFUL FOR: _____
_____

JOURNAL AREA

DATE:_____ TIME:_____

_____
_____
_____
_____
_____
_____
_____

MY PRAYER TIME

DATE:_____ TIME:_____

BIBLE PASSAGES & SCRIPTURES: _____
_____

WHAT GOD IS SAYING: _____
_____

WHAT I'M THANKFUL FOR: _____
_____

JOURNAL AREA

DATE:_____ TIME:_____

_____
_____
_____
_____
_____
_____
_____
_____

MY PRAYER TIME

DATE:_____ TIME:_____

BIBLE PASSAGES & SCRIPTURES: _____
_____

WHAT GOD IS SAYING: _____
_____

WHAT I'M THANKFUL FOR: _____
_____

JOURNAL AREA

DATE:_____ TIME:_____

_____
_____
_____
_____
_____
_____
_____

MY PRAYER TIME

DATE:_____ TIME:_____

BIBLE PASSAGES & SCRIPTURES: _____
_____

WHAT GOD IS SAYING: _____
_____

WHAT I'M THANKFUL FOR: _____
_____

JOURNAL AREA

DATE:_____ TIME:_____

_____
_____
_____
_____
_____
_____
_____

MY PRAYER TIME

DATE:_____ TIME:_____

BIBLE PASSAGES & SCRIPTURES: _____
_____

WHAT GOD IS SAYING: _____
_____

WHAT I'M THANKFUL FOR: _____
_____

JOURNAL AREA

DATE:_____ TIME:_____

_____
_____
_____
_____
_____
_____
_____

MY PRAYER TIME

DATE:_____ TIME:_____

BIBLE PASSAGES & SCRIPTURES: _____
_____

WHAT GOD IS SAYING: _____
_____

WHAT I'M THANKFUL FOR: _____
_____

JOURNAL AREA

DATE:_____ TIME:_____

_____
_____
_____
_____
_____
_____
_____

MY PRAYER TIME

DATE:_____ TIME:_____

BIBLE PASSAGES & SCRIPTURES: _____
_____

WHAT GOD IS SAYING: _____
_____

WHAT I'M THANKFUL FOR: _____
_____

JOURNAL AREA

DATE:_____ TIME:_____

_____
_____
_____
_____
_____
_____
_____

MY PRAYER TIME

DATE:_____ TIME:_____

BIBLE PASSAGES & SCRIPTURES: _____
_____

WHAT GOD IS SAYING: _____
_____

WHAT I'M THANKFUL FOR: _____
_____

JOURNAL AREA

DATE:_____ TIME:_____

_____
_____
_____
_____
_____
_____
_____

MY PRAYER TIME

DATE:_____ TIME:_____

BIBLE PASSAGES & SCRIPTURES: _____
_____

WHAT GOD IS SAYING: _____
_____

WHAT I'M THANKFUL FOR: _____
_____

JOURNAL AREA

DATE:_____ TIME:_____

_____
_____
_____
_____
_____
_____
_____

MY PRAYER TIME

DATE:_____ TIME:_____

BIBLE PASSAGES & SCRIPTURES: _____
_____

WHAT GOD IS SAYING: _____
_____

WHAT I'M THANKFUL FOR: _____
_____

JOURNAL AREA

DATE:_____ TIME:_____

_____
_____
_____
_____
_____
_____
_____

MY PRAYER TIME

DATE:_____ TIME:_____

BIBLE PASSAGES & SCRIPTURES: _____
_____

WHAT GOD IS SAYING: _____
_____

WHAT I'M THANKFUL FOR: _____
_____

JOURNAL AREA

DATE:_____ TIME:_____

_____
_____
_____
_____
_____
_____
_____

MY PRAYER TIME

DATE:_____ TIME:_____

BIBLE PASSAGES & SCRIPTURES: _____
_____

WHAT GOD IS SAYING: _____
_____

WHAT I'M THANKFUL FOR: _____
_____

JOURNAL AREA

DATE:_____ TIME:_____

_____
_____
_____
_____
_____
_____
_____
_____

MY PRAYER TIME

DATE:_____ TIME:_____

BIBLE PASSAGES & SCRIPTURES: _____
_____

WHAT GOD IS SAYING: _____
_____

WHAT I'M THANKFUL FOR: _____
_____

JOURNAL AREA

DATE:_____ TIME:_____

_____
_____
_____
_____
_____
_____
_____

MY PRAYER TIME

DATE:_____ TIME:_____

BIBLE PASSAGES & SCRIPTURES: _____
_____

WHAT GOD IS SAYING: _____
_____

WHAT I'M THANKFUL FOR: _____
_____

JOURNAL AREA

DATE:_____ TIME:_____

_____
_____
_____
_____
_____
_____
_____

MY PRAYER TIME

DATE:_____ TIME:_____

BIBLE PASSAGES & SCRIPTURES: _____
_____

WHAT GOD IS SAYING: _____
_____

WHAT I'M THANKFUL FOR: _____
_____

JOURNAL AREA

DATE:_____ TIME:_____

_____
_____
_____
_____
_____
_____
_____
_____

MY PRAYER TIME

DATE:_____ TIME:_____

BIBLE PASSAGES & SCRIPTURES: _____
_____

WHAT GOD IS SAYING: _____
_____

WHAT I'M THANKFUL FOR: _____
_____

JOURNAL AREA

DATE:_____ TIME:_____

_____
_____
_____
_____
_____
_____
_____

MY PRAYER TIME

DATE:_____ TIME:_____

BIBLE PASSAGES & SCRIPTURES: _____
_____

WHAT GOD IS SAYING: _____
_____

WHAT I'M THANKFUL FOR: _____
_____

JOURNAL AREA

DATE:_____ TIME:_____

_____
_____
_____
_____
_____
_____
_____
_____

MY PRAYER TIME

DATE:_____ TIME:_____

BIBLE PASSAGES & SCRIPTURES: _____
_____

WHAT GOD IS SAYING: _____
_____

WHAT I'M THANKFUL FOR: _____
_____

JOURNAL AREA

DATE:_____ TIME:_____

_____
_____
_____
_____
_____
_____
_____

MY PRAYER TIME

DATE:_____ TIME:_____

BIBLE PASSAGES & SCRIPTURES: _____
_____

WHAT GOD IS SAYING: _____
_____

WHAT I'M THANKFUL FOR: _____
_____

JOURNAL AREA

DATE:_____ TIME:_____

_____
_____
_____
_____
_____
_____
_____

MY PRAYER TIME

DATE:_____ TIME:_____

BIBLE PASSAGES & SCRIPTURES: _____

_____

WHAT GOD IS SAYING: _____

_____

WHAT I'M THANKFUL FOR: _____

_____

JOURNAL AREA

DATE:_____ TIME:_____

_____

_____

_____

_____

_____

_____

_____

MY PRAYER TIME

DATE:_____ TIME:_____

BIBLE PASSAGES & SCRIPTURES: _____
_____

WHAT GOD IS SAYING: _____
_____

WHAT I'M THANKFUL FOR: _____
_____

JOURNAL AREA

DATE:_____ TIME:_____

_____
_____
_____
_____
_____
_____
_____

MY PRAYER TIME

DATE:_____ TIME:_____

BIBLE PASSAGES & SCRIPTURES: _____
_____

WHAT GOD IS SAYING: _____
_____

WHAT I'M THANKFUL FOR: _____
_____

JOURNAL AREA

DATE:_____ TIME:_____

_____
_____
_____
_____
_____
_____
_____

MY PRAYER TIME

DATE:_____ TIME:_____

BIBLE PASSAGES & SCRIPTURES: _____
_____

WHAT GOD IS SAYING: _____
_____

WHAT I'M THANKFUL FOR: _____
_____

JOURNAL AREA

DATE:_____ TIME:_____

_____
_____
_____
_____
_____
_____
_____

MY PRAYER TIME

DATE:_____ TIME:_____

BIBLE PASSAGES & SCRIPTURES: _____
_____

WHAT GOD IS SAYING: _____
_____

WHAT I'M THANKFUL FOR: _____
_____

JOURNAL AREA

DATE:_____ TIME:_____

_____
_____
_____
_____
_____
_____
_____

MY PRAYER TIME

DATE:_____ TIME:_____

BIBLE PASSAGES & SCRIPTURES: _____
_____

WHAT GOD IS SAYING: _____
_____

WHAT I'M THANKFUL FOR: _____
_____

JOURNAL AREA

DATE:_____ TIME:_____

_____
_____
_____
_____
_____
_____
_____

MY PRAYER TIME

DATE:_____ TIME:_____

BIBLE PASSAGES & SCRIPTURES: _____
_____

WHAT GOD IS SAYING: _____
_____

WHAT I'M THANKFUL FOR: _____
_____

JOURNAL AREA

DATE:_____ TIME:_____

_____
_____
_____
_____
_____
_____
_____

MY PRAYER TIME

DATE:_____ TIME:_____

BIBLE PASSAGES & SCRIPTURES: _____
_____

WHAT GOD IS SAYING: _____
_____

WHAT I'M THANKFUL FOR: _____
_____

JOURNAL AREA

DATE:_____ TIME:_____

_____
_____
_____
_____
_____
_____
_____

MY PRAYER TIME

DATE:_____   TIME:_____

BIBLE PASSAGES & SCRIPTURES: _____
_____

WHAT GOD IS SAYING: _____
_____

WHAT I'M THANKFUL FOR: _____
_____

JOURNAL AREA

DATE:_____   TIME:_____

_____
_____
_____
_____
_____
_____
_____

MY PRAYER TIME

DATE:_____ TIME:_____

BIBLE PASSAGES & SCRIPTURES: _____
_____

WHAT GOD IS SAYING: _____
_____

WHAT I'M THANKFUL FOR: _____
_____

JOURNAL AREA

DATE:_____ TIME:_____

_____
_____
_____
_____
_____
_____
_____
_____

MY PRAYER TIME

DATE:_____ TIME:_____

BIBLE PASSAGES & SCRIPTURES: _____
_____

WHAT GOD IS SAYING: _____
_____

WHAT I'M THANKFUL FOR: _____
_____

JOURNAL AREA

DATE:_____ TIME:_____

_____
_____
_____
_____
_____
_____
_____

MY PRAYER TIME

DATE:_____ TIME:_____

BIBLE PASSAGES & SCRIPTURES: _____
_____

WHAT GOD IS SAYING: _____
_____

WHAT I'M THANKFUL FOR: _____
_____

JOURNAL AREA

DATE:_____ TIME:_____

_____
_____
_____
_____
_____
_____
_____

MY PRAYER TIME

DATE:_____ TIME:_____

BIBLE PASSAGES & SCRIPTURES: _____
_____

WHAT GOD IS SAYING: _____
_____

WHAT I'M THANKFUL FOR: _____
_____

JOURNAL AREA

DATE:_____ TIME:_____

_____
_____
_____
_____
_____
_____
_____

MY PRAYER TIME

DATE:_____ TIME:_____

BIBLE PASSAGES & SCRIPTURES: _____
_____

WHAT GOD IS SAYING: _____
_____

WHAT I'M THANKFUL FOR: _____
_____

JOURNAL AREA

DATE:_____ TIME:_____

_____
_____
_____
_____
_____
_____
_____
_____

MY PRAYER TIME

DATE:_____ TIME:_____

BIBLE PASSAGES & SCRIPTURES: _____
_____

WHAT GOD IS SAYING: _____
_____

WHAT I'M THANKFUL FOR: _____
_____

JOURNAL AREA

DATE:_____ TIME:_____

_____
_____
_____
_____
_____
_____
_____

MY PRAYER TIME

DATE:_____ TIME:_____

BIBLE PASSAGES & SCRIPTURES: _____
_____

WHAT GOD IS SAYING: _____
_____

WHAT I'M THANKFUL FOR: _____
_____

JOURNAL AREA

DATE:_____ TIME:_____

_____
_____
_____
_____
_____
_____
_____

MY PRAYER TIME

DATE:_____ TIME:_____

BIBLE PASSAGES & SCRIPTURES: _____
_____

WHAT GOD IS SAYING: _____
_____

WHAT I'M THANKFUL FOR: _____
_____

JOURNAL AREA

DATE:_____ TIME:_____

_____
_____
_____
_____
_____
_____
_____

MY PRAYER TIME

DATE:_____ TIME:_____

BIBLE PASSAGES & SCRIPTURES: _____
_____

WHAT GOD IS SAYING: _____
_____

WHAT I'M THANKFUL FOR: _____
_____

JOURNAL AREA

DATE:_____ TIME:_____

_____
_____
_____
_____
_____
_____
_____
_____

MY PRAYER TIME

DATE:_____ TIME:_____

BIBLE PASSAGES & SCRIPTURES: _____
_____

WHAT GOD IS SAYING: _____
_____

WHAT I'M THANKFUL FOR: _____
_____

JOURNAL AREA

DATE:_____ TIME:_____

_____
_____
_____
_____
_____
_____
_____

MY PRAYER TIME

DATE:_____ TIME:_____

BIBLE PASSAGES & SCRIPTURES: _____
_____

WHAT GOD IS SAYING: _____
_____

WHAT I'M THANKFUL FOR: _____
_____

JOURNAL AREA

DATE:_____ TIME:_____

_____
_____
_____
_____
_____
_____
_____

MY PRAYER TIME

DATE:_____   TIME:_____

BIBLE PASSAGES & SCRIPTURES: _____
_____

WHAT GOD IS SAYING: _____
_____

WHAT I'M THANKFUL FOR: _____
_____

JOURNAL AREA

DATE:_____   TIME:_____

_____
_____
_____
_____
_____
_____
_____

MY PRAYER TIME

DATE:_____ TIME:_____

BIBLE PASSAGES & SCRIPTURES: _____
_____

WHAT GOD IS SAYING: _____
_____

WHAT I'M THANKFUL FOR: _____
_____

JOURNAL AREA

DATE:_____ TIME:_____

_____
_____
_____
_____
_____
_____
_____
_____

MY PRAYER TIME

DATE:_____ TIME:_____

BIBLE PASSAGES & SCRIPTURES: _____
_____

WHAT GOD IS SAYING: _____
_____

WHAT I'M THANKFUL FOR: _____
_____

JOURNAL AREA

DATE:_____ TIME:_____

_____
_____
_____
_____
_____
_____
_____

MY PRAYER TIME

DATE:_____ TIME:_____

BIBLE PASSAGES & SCRIPTURES: _____
_____

WHAT GOD IS SAYING: _____
_____

WHAT I'M THANKFUL FOR: _____
_____

JOURNAL AREA

DATE:_____ TIME:_____

_____
_____
_____
_____
_____
_____
_____
_____

MY PRAYER TIME

DATE:_____ TIME:_____

BIBLE PASSAGES & SCRIPTURES: _____
_____

WHAT GOD IS SAYING: _____
_____

WHAT I'M THANKFUL FOR: _____
_____

JOURNAL AREA

DATE:_____ TIME:_____

_____
_____
_____
_____
_____
_____
_____

MY PRAYER TIME

DATE:_____ TIME:_____

BIBLE PASSAGES & SCRIPTURES: _____
_____

WHAT GOD IS SAYING: _____
_____

WHAT I'M THANKFUL FOR: _____
_____

JOURNAL AREA

DATE:_____ TIME:_____

_____
_____
_____
_____
_____
_____
_____

MY PRAYER TIME

DATE:_____ TIME:_____

BIBLE PASSAGES & SCRIPTURES: _____
_____

WHAT GOD IS SAYING: _____
_____

WHAT I'M THANKFUL FOR: _____
_____

JOURNAL AREA

DATE:_____ TIME:_____

_____
_____
_____
_____
_____
_____
_____

MY PRAYER TIME

DATE:_____ TIME:_____

BIBLE PASSAGES & SCRIPTURES: _____
_____

WHAT GOD IS SAYING: _____
_____

WHAT I'M THANKFUL FOR: _____
_____

JOURNAL AREA

DATE:_____ TIME:_____

_____
_____
_____
_____
_____
_____
_____

MY PRAYER TIME

DATE:_____ TIME:_____

BIBLE PASSAGES & SCRIPTURES: _____
_____

WHAT GOD IS SAYING: _____
_____

WHAT I'M THANKFUL FOR: _____
_____

JOURNAL AREA

DATE:_____ TIME:_____

_____
_____
_____
_____
_____
_____
_____

MY PRAYER TIME

DATE:_____ TIME:_____

BIBLE PASSAGES & SCRIPTURES: _____
_____

WHAT GOD IS SAYING: _____
_____

WHAT I'M THANKFUL FOR: _____
_____

JOURNAL AREA

DATE:_____ TIME:_____

_____
_____
_____
_____
_____
_____
_____
_____

MY PRAYER TIME

DATE:_____ TIME:_____

BIBLE PASSAGES & SCRIPTURES: _____
_____

WHAT GOD IS SAYING: _____
_____

WHAT I'M THANKFUL FOR: _____
_____

JOURNAL AREA

DATE:_____ TIME:_____

_____
_____
_____
_____
_____
_____
_____

MY PRAYER TIME

DATE:_____ TIME:_____

BIBLE PASSAGES & SCRIPTURES: _____
_____

WHAT GOD IS SAYING: _____
_____

WHAT I'M THANKFUL FOR: _____
_____

JOURNAL AREA

DATE:_____ TIME:_____

_____
_____
_____
_____
_____
_____
_____

MY PRAYER TIME

DATE:_____   TIME:_____

BIBLE PASSAGES & SCRIPTURES: _____
_____

WHAT GOD IS SAYING: _____
_____

WHAT I'M THANKFUL FOR: _____
_____

JOURNAL AREA

DATE:_____   TIME:_____

_____
_____
_____
_____
_____
_____
_____

MY PRAYER TIME

DATE:_____ TIME:_____

BIBLE PASSAGES & SCRIPTURES: _____
_____

WHAT GOD IS SAYING: _____
_____

WHAT I'M THANKFUL FOR: _____
_____

JOURNAL AREA

DATE:_____ TIME:_____

_____
_____
_____
_____
_____
_____
_____
_____

MY PRAYER TIME

DATE:_____ TIME:_____

BIBLE PASSAGES & SCRIPTURES: _____
_____

WHAT GOD IS SAYING: _____
_____

WHAT I'M THANKFUL FOR: _____
_____

JOURNAL AREA

DATE:_____ TIME:_____

_____
_____
_____
_____
_____
_____
_____

MY PRAYER TIME

DATE:_____ TIME:_____

BIBLE PASSAGES & SCRIPTURES: _____
_____

WHAT GOD IS SAYING: _____
_____

WHAT I'M THANKFUL FOR: _____
_____

JOURNAL AREA

DATE:_____ TIME:_____

_____
_____
_____
_____
_____
_____
_____

MY PRAYER TIME

DATE:_____ TIME:_____

BIBLE PASSAGES & SCRIPTURES: _____
_____

WHAT GOD IS SAYING: _____
_____

WHAT I'M THANKFUL FOR: _____
_____

JOURNAL AREA

DATE:_____ TIME:_____

_____
_____
_____
_____
_____
_____
_____

MY PRAYER TIME

DATE:_____ TIME:_____

BIBLE PASSAGES & SCRIPTURES: _____
_____

WHAT GOD IS SAYING: _____
_____

WHAT I'M THANKFUL FOR: _____
_____

JOURNAL AREA

DATE:_____ TIME:_____

_____
_____
_____
_____
_____
_____
_____

MY PRAYER TIME

DATE:_____ TIME:_____

BIBLE PASSAGES & SCRIPTURES: _____
_____

WHAT GOD IS SAYING: _____
_____

WHAT I'M THANKFUL FOR: _____
_____

JOURNAL AREA

DATE:_____ TIME:_____

_____
_____
_____
_____
_____
_____
_____

MY PRAYER TIME

DATE:_____ TIME:_____

BIBLE PASSAGES & SCRIPTURES: _____
_____

WHAT GOD IS SAYING: _____
_____

WHAT I'M THANKFUL FOR: _____
_____

JOURNAL AREA

DATE:_____ TIME:_____

_____
_____
_____
_____
_____
_____
_____

MY PRAYER TIME

DATE:_____ TIME:_____

BIBLE PASSAGES & SCRIPTURES: _____
_____

WHAT GOD IS SAYING: _____
_____

WHAT I'M THANKFUL FOR: _____
_____

JOURNAL AREA

DATE:_____ TIME:_____

_____
_____
_____
_____
_____
_____
_____

MY PRAYER TIME

DATE:_____ TIME:_____

BIBLE PASSAGES & SCRIPTURES: _____
_____

WHAT GOD IS SAYING: _____
_____

WHAT I'M THANKFUL FOR: _____
_____

JOURNAL AREA

DATE:_____ TIME:_____

_____
_____
_____
_____
_____
_____
_____

MY PRAYER TIME

DATE:_____ TIME:_____

BIBLE PASSAGES & SCRIPTURES: _____
_____

WHAT GOD IS SAYING: _____
_____

WHAT I'M THANKFUL FOR: _____
_____

JOURNAL AREA

DATE:_____ TIME:_____

_____
_____
_____
_____
_____
_____
_____

MY PRAYER TIME

DATE:_____ TIME:_____

BIBLE PASSAGES & SCRIPTURES: _____
_____

WHAT GOD IS SAYING: _____
_____

WHAT I'M THANKFUL FOR: _____
_____

JOURNAL AREA

DATE:_____ TIME:_____

_____
_____
_____
_____
_____
_____
_____

MY PRAYER TIME

DATE:_____   TIME:_____

BIBLE PASSAGES & SCRIPTURES: _____
_____

WHAT GOD IS SAYING: _____
_____

WHAT I'M THANKFUL FOR: _____
_____

JOURNAL AREA

DATE:_____   TIME:_____

_____
_____
_____
_____
_____
_____
_____

MY PRAYER TIME

DATE:_____ TIME:_____

BIBLE PASSAGES & SCRIPTURES: _____
_____

WHAT GOD IS SAYING: _____
_____

WHAT I'M THANKFUL FOR: _____
_____

JOURNAL AREA

DATE:_____ TIME:_____

_____
_____
_____
_____
_____
_____
_____

MY PRAYER TIME

DATE:_____ TIME:_____

BIBLE PASSAGES & SCRIPTURES: _____
_____

WHAT GOD IS SAYING: _____
_____

WHAT I'M THANKFUL FOR: _____
_____

JOURNAL AREA

DATE:_____ TIME:_____

_____
_____
_____
_____
_____
_____
_____

MY PRAYER TIME

DATE:_____ TIME:_____

BIBLE PASSAGES & SCRIPTURES: _____
_____

WHAT GOD IS SAYING: _____
_____

WHAT I'M THANKFUL FOR: _____
_____

JOURNAL AREA

DATE:_____ TIME:_____

_____
_____
_____
_____
_____
_____
_____

MY PRAYER TIME

DATE:_____ TIME:_____

BIBLE PASSAGES & SCRIPTURES: _____
_____

WHAT GOD IS SAYING: _____
_____

WHAT I'M THANKFUL FOR: _____
_____

JOURNAL AREA

DATE:_____ TIME:_____

_____
_____
_____
_____
_____
_____
_____

MY PRAYER TIME

DATE:_____ TIME:_____

BIBLE PASSAGES & SCRIPTURES: _____

_____

WHAT GOD IS SAYING: _____

_____

WHAT I'M THANKFUL FOR: _____

_____

JOURNAL AREA

DATE:_____ TIME:_____

_____

_____

_____

_____

_____

_____

_____

MY PRAYER TIME

DATE:_____ TIME:_____

BIBLE PASSAGES & SCRIPTURES: _____
_____

WHAT GOD IS SAYING: _____
_____

WHAT I'M THANKFUL FOR: _____
_____

JOURNAL AREA

DATE:_____ TIME:_____

_____
_____
_____
_____
_____
_____
_____

MY PRAYER TIME

DATE:_____ TIME:_____

BIBLE PASSAGES & SCRIPTURES: _____
_____

WHAT GOD IS SAYING: _____
_____

WHAT I'M THANKFUL FOR: _____
_____

JOURNAL AREA

DATE:_____ TIME:_____

_____
_____
_____
_____
_____
_____
_____

MY PRAYER TIME

DATE:_____ TIME:_____

BIBLE PASSAGES & SCRIPTURES: _____
_____

WHAT GOD IS SAYING: _____
_____

WHAT I'M THANKFUL FOR: _____
_____

JOURNAL AREA

DATE:_____ TIME:_____

_____
_____
_____
_____
_____
_____
_____

MY PRAYER TIME

DATE:_____ TIME:_____

BIBLE PASSAGES & SCRIPTURES: _____
_____

WHAT GOD IS SAYING: _____
_____

WHAT I'M THANKFUL FOR: _____
_____

JOURNAL AREA

DATE:_____ TIME:_____

_____
_____
_____
_____
_____
_____
_____

MY PRAYER TIME

DATE:_____ TIME:_____

BIBLE PASSAGES & SCRIPTURES: _____
_____

WHAT GOD IS SAYING: _____
_____

WHAT I'M THANKFUL FOR: _____
_____

JOURNAL AREA

DATE:_____ TIME:_____

_____
_____
_____
_____
_____
_____
_____

MY PRAYER TIME

DATE:_____ TIME:_____

BIBLE PASSAGES & SCRIPTURES: _____
_____

WHAT GOD IS SAYING: _____
_____

WHAT I'M THANKFUL FOR: _____
_____

JOURNAL AREA

DATE:_____ TIME:_____

_____
_____
_____
_____
_____
_____
_____

MY PRAYER TIME

DATE:_____ TIME:_____

BIBLE PASSAGES & SCRIPTURES: _____
_____

WHAT GOD IS SAYING: _____
_____

WHAT I'M THANKFUL FOR: _____
_____

JOURNAL AREA

DATE:_____ TIME:_____

_____
_____
_____
_____
_____
_____
_____

MY PRAYER TIME

DATE:_____ TIME:_____

BIBLE PASSAGES & SCRIPTURES: _____
_____

WHAT GOD IS SAYING: _____
_____

WHAT I'M THANKFUL FOR: _____
_____

JOURNAL AREA

DATE:_____ TIME:_____

_____
_____
_____
_____
_____
_____
_____

MY PRAYER TIME

DATE:_____ TIME:_____

BIBLE PASSAGES & SCRIPTURES: _____
_____

WHAT GOD IS SAYING: _____
_____

WHAT I'M THANKFUL FOR: _____
_____

JOURNAL AREA

DATE:_____ TIME:_____

_____
_____
_____
_____
_____
_____
_____

MY PRAYER TIME

DATE:_____   TIME:_____

BIBLE PASSAGES & SCRIPTURES: _____
_____

WHAT GOD IS SAYING: _____
_____

WHAT I'M THANKFUL FOR: _____
_____

JOURNAL AREA

DATE:_____   TIME:_____

_____
_____
_____
_____
_____
_____
_____

MY PRAYER TIME

DATE:_____ TIME:_____

BIBLE PASSAGES & SCRIPTURES: _____
_____

WHAT GOD IS SAYING: _____
_____

WHAT I'M THANKFUL FOR: _____
_____

JOURNAL AREA

DATE:_____ TIME:_____

_____
_____
_____
_____
_____
_____
_____

MY PRAYER TIME

DATE:_____ TIME:_____

BIBLE PASSAGES & SCRIPTURES: _____
_____

WHAT GOD IS SAYING: _____
_____

WHAT I'M THANKFUL FOR: _____
_____

JOURNAL AREA

DATE:_____ TIME:_____

_____
_____
_____
_____
_____
_____
_____
_____

MY PRAYER TIME

DATE:_____ TIME:_____

BIBLE PASSAGES & SCRIPTURES: _____
_____

WHAT GOD IS SAYING: _____
_____

WHAT I'M THANKFUL FOR: _____
_____

JOURNAL AREA

DATE:_____ TIME:_____

_____
_____
_____
_____
_____
_____
_____
_____

MY PRAYER TIME

DATE:_____ TIME:_____

BIBLE PASSAGES & SCRIPTURES: _____
_____

WHAT GOD IS SAYING: _____
_____

WHAT I'M THANKFUL FOR: _____
_____

JOURNAL AREA

DATE:_____ TIME:_____

_____
_____
_____
_____
_____
_____
_____

MY PRAYER TIME

DATE:_____ TIME:_____

BIBLE PASSAGES & SCRIPTURES: _____
_____

WHAT GOD IS SAYING: _____
_____

WHAT I'M THANKFUL FOR: _____
_____

JOURNAL AREA

DATE:_____ TIME:_____

_____
_____
_____
_____
_____
_____
_____

MY PRAYER TIME

DATE:_____ TIME:_____

BIBLE PASSAGES & SCRIPTURES: _____
_____

WHAT GOD IS SAYING: _____
_____

WHAT I'M THANKFUL FOR: _____
_____

JOURNAL AREA

DATE:_____ TIME:_____

_____
_____
_____
_____
_____
_____
_____

MY PRAYER TIME

DATE:_____ TIME:_____

BIBLE PASSAGES & SCRIPTURES: _____
_____

WHAT GOD IS SAYING: _____
_____

WHAT I'M THANKFUL FOR: _____
_____

JOURNAL AREA

DATE:_____ TIME:_____

_____
_____
_____
_____
_____
_____
_____

MY PRAYER TIME

DATE:_____ TIME:_____

BIBLE PASSAGES & SCRIPTURES: _____
_____

WHAT GOD IS SAYING: _____
_____

WHAT I'M THANKFUL FOR: _____
_____

JOURNAL AREA

DATE:_____ TIME:_____

_____
_____
_____
_____
_____
_____
_____

MY PRAYER TIME

DATE:_____ TIME:_____

BIBLE PASSAGES & SCRIPTURES: _____
_____

WHAT GOD IS SAYING: _____
_____

WHAT I'M THANKFUL FOR: _____
_____

JOURNAL AREA

DATE:_____ TIME:_____

_____
_____
_____
_____
_____
_____
_____

MY PRAYER TIME

DATE:_____ TIME:_____

BIBLE PASSAGES & SCRIPTURES: _____
_____

WHAT GOD IS SAYING: _____
_____

WHAT I'M THANKFUL FOR: _____
_____

JOURNAL AREA

DATE:_____ TIME:_____

_____
_____
_____
_____
_____
_____
_____

MY PRAYER TIME

DATE:_____ TIME:_____

BIBLE PASSAGES & SCRIPTURES: _____
_____

WHAT GOD IS SAYING: _____
_____

WHAT I'M THANKFUL FOR: _____
_____

JOURNAL AREA

DATE:_____ TIME:_____

_____
_____
_____
_____
_____
_____
_____

MY PRAYER TIME

DATE:_____ TIME:_____

BIBLE PASSAGES & SCRIPTURES: _____
_____

WHAT GOD IS SAYING: _____
_____

WHAT I'M THANKFUL FOR: _____
_____

JOURNAL AREA

DATE:_____ TIME:_____

_____
_____
_____
_____
_____
_____
_____

MY PRAYER TIME

DATE:_____ TIME:_____

BIBLE PASSAGES & SCRIPTURES: _____
_____

WHAT GOD IS SAYING: _____
_____

WHAT I'M THANKFUL FOR: _____
_____

JOURNAL AREA

DATE:_____ TIME:_____

_____
_____
_____
_____
_____
_____
_____

MY PRAYER TIME

DATE:_____ TIME:_____

BIBLE PASSAGES & SCRIPTURES: _____
_____

WHAT GOD IS SAYING: _____
_____

WHAT I'M THANKFUL FOR: _____
_____

JOURNAL AREA

DATE:_____ TIME:_____

_____
_____
_____
_____
_____
_____
_____

MY PRAYER TIME

DATE:_____ TIME:_____

BIBLE PASSAGES & SCRIPTURES: _____
_____

WHAT GOD IS SAYING: _____
_____

WHAT I'M THANKFUL FOR: _____
_____

JOURNAL AREA

DATE:_____ TIME:_____

_____
_____
_____
_____
_____
_____
_____

MY PRAYER TIME

DATE:_____ TIME:_____

BIBLE PASSAGES & SCRIPTURES: _____
_____

WHAT GOD IS SAYING: _____
_____

WHAT I'M THANKFUL FOR: _____
_____

JOURNAL AREA

DATE:_____ TIME:_____

_____
_____
_____
_____
_____
_____
_____

MY PRAYER TIME

DATE:_____ TIME:_____

BIBLE PASSAGES & SCRIPTURES: _____
_____

WHAT GOD IS SAYING: _____
_____

WHAT I'M THANKFUL FOR: _____
_____

JOURNAL AREA

DATE:_____ TIME:_____

_____
_____
_____
_____
_____
_____
_____

MY PRAYER TIME

DATE:_____ TIME:_____

BIBLE PASSAGES & SCRIPTURES: _____
_____

WHAT GOD IS SAYING: _____
_____

WHAT I'M THANKFUL FOR: _____
_____

JOURNAL AREA

DATE:_____ TIME:_____

_____
_____
_____
_____
_____
_____
_____
_____

MY PRAYER TIME

DATE:_____ TIME:_____

BIBLE PASSAGES & SCRIPTURES: _____
_____

WHAT GOD IS SAYING: _____
_____

WHAT I'M THANKFUL FOR: _____
_____

JOURNAL AREA

DATE:_____ TIME:_____

_____
_____
_____
_____
_____
_____
_____

MY PRAYER TIME

DATE:_____ TIME:_____

BIBLE PASSAGES & SCRIPTURES: _____
_____

WHAT GOD IS SAYING: _____
_____

WHAT I'M THANKFUL FOR: _____
_____

JOURNAL AREA

DATE:_____ TIME:_____

_____
_____
_____
_____
_____
_____
_____
_____

MY PRAYER TIME

DATE:_____ TIME:_____

BIBLE PASSAGES & SCRIPTURES: _____
_____

WHAT GOD IS SAYING: _____
_____

WHAT I'M THANKFUL FOR: _____
_____

JOURNAL AREA

DATE:_____ TIME:_____

_____
_____
_____
_____
_____
_____
_____

MY PRAYER TIME

DATE:_____ TIME:_____

BIBLE PASSAGES & SCRIPTURES: _____
_____

WHAT GOD IS SAYING: _____
_____

WHAT I'M THANKFUL FOR: _____
_____

JOURNAL AREA

DATE:_____ TIME:_____

_____
_____
_____
_____
_____
_____
_____

MY PRAYER TIME

DATE:_____ TIME:_____

BIBLE PASSAGES & SCRIPTURES: _____
_____

WHAT GOD IS SAYING: _____
_____

WHAT I'M THANKFUL FOR: _____
_____

JOURNAL AREA

DATE:_____ TIME:_____

_____
_____
_____
_____
_____
_____
_____

MY PRAYER TIME

DATE:_____ TIME:_____

BIBLE PASSAGES & SCRIPTURES: _____
_____

WHAT GOD IS SAYING: _____
_____

WHAT I'M THANKFUL FOR: _____
_____

JOURNAL AREA

DATE:_____ TIME:_____

_____
_____
_____
_____
_____
_____
_____
_____

MY PRAYER TIME

DATE:_____ TIME:_____

BIBLE PASSAGES & SCRIPTURES: _____
_____

WHAT GOD IS SAYING: _____
_____

WHAT I'M THANKFUL FOR: _____
_____

JOURNAL AREA

DATE:_____ TIME:_____

_____
_____
_____
_____
_____
_____
_____

MY PRAYER TIME

DATE:_____ TIME:_____

BIBLE PASSAGES & SCRIPTURES: _____
_____

WHAT GOD IS SAYING: _____
_____

WHAT I'M THANKFUL FOR: _____
_____

JOURNAL AREA

DATE:_____ TIME:_____

_____
_____
_____
_____
_____
_____
_____

MY PRAYER TIME

DATE:_____ TIME:_____

BIBLE PASSAGES & SCRIPTURES: _____
_____

WHAT GOD IS SAYING: _____
_____

WHAT I'M THANKFUL FOR: _____
_____

JOURNAL AREA

DATE:_____ TIME:_____

_____
_____
_____
_____
_____
_____
_____

MY PRAYER TIME

DATE:_____ TIME:_____

BIBLE PASSAGES & SCRIPTURES: _____
_____

WHAT GOD IS SAYING: _____
_____

WHAT I'M THANKFUL FOR: _____
_____

JOURNAL AREA

DATE:_____ TIME:_____

_____
_____
_____
_____
_____
_____
_____
_____

MY PRAYER TIME

DATE:_____ TIME:_____

BIBLE PASSAGES & SCRIPTURES: _____
_____

WHAT GOD IS SAYING: _____
_____

WHAT I'M THANKFUL FOR: _____
_____

JOURNAL AREA

DATE:_____ TIME:_____

_____
_____
_____
_____
_____
_____
_____

MY PRAYER TIME

DATE:_____ TIME:_____

BIBLE PASSAGES & SCRIPTURES: _____
_____

WHAT GOD IS SAYING: _____
_____

WHAT I'M THANKFUL FOR: _____
_____

JOURNAL AREA

DATE:_____ TIME:_____

_____
_____
_____
_____
_____
_____
_____
_____

MY PRAYER TIME

DATE:_____ TIME:_____

BIBLE PASSAGES & SCRIPTURES: _____
_____

WHAT GOD IS SAYING: _____
_____

WHAT I'M THANKFUL FOR: _____
_____

JOURNAL AREA

DATE:_____ TIME:_____

_____
_____
_____
_____
_____
_____
_____

MY PRAYER TIME

DATE:_____ TIME:_____

BIBLE PASSAGES & SCRIPTURES: _____
_____

WHAT GOD IS SAYING: _____
_____

WHAT I'M THANKFUL FOR: _____
_____

JOURNAL AREA

DATE:_____ TIME:_____

_____
_____
_____
_____
_____
_____
_____

MY PRAYER TIME

DATE:_____   TIME:_____

BIBLE PASSAGES & SCRIPTURES: _____
_____

WHAT GOD IS SAYING: _____
_____

WHAT I'M THANKFUL FOR: _____
_____

JOURNAL AREA

DATE:_____   TIME:_____

_____
_____
_____
_____
_____
_____
_____

MY PRAYER TIME

DATE:_____ TIME:_____

BIBLE PASSAGES & SCRIPTURES: _____
_____

WHAT GOD IS SAYING: _____
_____

WHAT I'M THANKFUL FOR: _____
_____

JOURNAL AREA

DATE:_____ TIME:_____

_____
_____
_____
_____
_____
_____
_____

MY PRAYER TIME

DATE:_____ TIME:_____

BIBLE PASSAGES & SCRIPTURES: _____
_____

WHAT GOD IS SAYING: _____
_____

WHAT I'M THANKFUL FOR: _____
_____

JOURNAL AREA

DATE:_____ TIME:_____

_____
_____
_____
_____
_____
_____
_____

MY PRAYER TIME

DATE:_____ TIME:_____

BIBLE PASSAGES & SCRIPTURES: _____
_____

WHAT GOD IS SAYING: _____
_____

WHAT I'M THANKFUL FOR: _____
_____

JOURNAL AREA

DATE:_____ TIME:_____

_____
_____
_____
_____
_____
_____
_____

MY PRAYER TIME

DATE:_____ TIME:_____

BIBLE PASSAGES & SCRIPTURES: _____
_____

WHAT GOD IS SAYING: _____
_____

WHAT I'M THANKFUL FOR: _____
_____

JOURNAL AREA

DATE:_____ TIME:_____

_____
_____
_____
_____
_____
_____
_____

MY PRAYER TIME

DATE:_____ TIME:_____

BIBLE PASSAGES & SCRIPTURES: _____
_____

WHAT GOD IS SAYING: _____
_____

WHAT I'M THANKFUL FOR: _____
_____

JOURNAL AREA

DATE:_____ TIME:_____

_____
_____
_____
_____
_____
_____
_____
_____

MY PRAYER TIME

DATE:_____ TIME:_____

BIBLE PASSAGES & SCRIPTURES: _____
_____

WHAT GOD IS SAYING: _____
_____

WHAT I'M THANKFUL FOR: _____
_____

JOURNAL AREA

DATE:_____ TIME:_____

_____
_____
_____
_____
_____
_____
_____

MY PRAYER TIME

DATE:_____   TIME:_____

BIBLE PASSAGES & SCRIPTURES: _____
_____

WHAT GOD IS SAYING: _____
_____

WHAT I'M THANKFUL FOR: _____
_____

JOURNAL AREA

DATE:_____   TIME:_____

_____
_____
_____
_____
_____
_____
_____

MY PRAYER TIME

DATE:_____ TIME:_____

BIBLE PASSAGES & SCRIPTURES: _____
_____

WHAT GOD IS SAYING: _____
_____

WHAT I'M THANKFUL FOR: _____
_____

JOURNAL AREA

DATE:_____ TIME:_____

_____
_____
_____
_____
_____
_____
_____

MY PRAYER TIME

DATE:_____ TIME:_____

BIBLE PASSAGES & SCRIPTURES: _____
_____

WHAT GOD IS SAYING: _____
_____

WHAT I'M THANKFUL FOR: _____
_____

JOURNAL AREA

DATE:_____ TIME:_____

_____
_____
_____
_____
_____
_____
_____

MY PRAYER TIME

DATE:_____ TIME:_____

BIBLE PASSAGES & SCRIPTURES: _____
_____

WHAT GOD IS SAYING: _____
_____

WHAT I'M THANKFUL FOR: _____
_____

JOURNAL AREA

DATE:_____ TIME:_____

_____
_____
_____
_____
_____
_____
_____

MY PRAYER TIME

DATE:_____ TIME:_____

BIBLE PASSAGES & SCRIPTURES: _____
_____

WHAT GOD IS SAYING: _____
_____

WHAT I'M THANKFUL FOR: _____
_____

JOURNAL AREA

DATE:_____ TIME:_____

_____
_____
_____
_____
_____
_____
_____
_____

THE BATTLEFIELD OF INTERCESSORS

RESOURCE SECTION
8 TYPES OF PRAYER

RESOURCE SECTION
8 TYPES OF PRAYER

PRAYER OF FAITH. THE PRAYER OF PETITION, OR TO CHANGE THINGS.

"And all things, whatsoever ye shall ask in prayer, believing, ye shall receive." - Matt 21:22 KJV

Prayer of Consecration. The prayer of dedication, or to be set apart by God for His purposes.
"As they ministered to the Lord, and fasted, the Holy Ghost said, Separate me Barnabas and Saul for the work whereunto I have called them." - Acts 13:2 KJV

"Saying, Father, if thou be willing, remove this cup from me: nevertheless not my will, but thine, be done." - Luke 22:42 KJV

PRAYER OF COMMITMENT. THE PRAYER OF COMMITTING A PERSON, EVENT OR CIRCUMSTANCE TO GOD; THE ACT OF LAYING THAT PERSON, EVENT OR CIRCUMSTANCE ASIDE AS A BURDEN THAT MUST BE RELEASED.

"Casting all your care upon him; for he careth for you." - 1 Peter 5:7 KJV

PRAYER OF WORSHIP. THE PSALMS ARE FULL OF PRAYERS OF WORSHIP EXTOLLING GOD.
PRAYER IN AGREEMENT.

"Again I say unto you, That if two of you shall agree on earth as touching any thing that they shall ask, it shall be done for them of my Father which is in heaven. For where two or three are gathered together in my name, there am I in the midst of them." - Matthew 18:19-20 KJV

RESOURCE SECTION
8 TYPES OF PRAYER

PRAYER IN THE SPIRIT
"For he that speaketh in an unknown tongue speaketh not unto men, but unto God: for no man understandeth him; howbeit in the spirit he speaketh mysteries." - 1 Corinthians 14:2 KJV

"For if I pray in an unknown tongue, my spirit prayeth, but my understanding is unfruitful. What is it then? I will pray with the spirit, and I will pray with the understanding also: I will sing with the spirit, and I will sing with the understanding also." -1 Corinthians 14-15 KJV

UNITED PRAYER
"And when they had prayed, the place was shaken where they were assembled together; and they were all filled with the Holy Ghost, and they spake the word of God with boldness." - Acts 4:23-30 & 31 KJV

INTERCESSORY PRAYER
"Who is he that condemneth? It is Christ that died, yea rather, that is risen again, who is even at the right hand of God, who also maketh intercession for us." - Rom 8:34 KJV

"And the LORD appeared to Solomon by night, and said unto him, I have heard thy prayer, and have chosen this place to myself for an house of sacrifice. 13If I shut up heaven that there be no rain, or if I command the locusts to devour the land, or if I send pestilence among my people; 14If my people, which are called by my name, shall humble themselves, and pray, and seek my face, and turn from their wicked ways; then will I hear from heaven, and will forgive their sin, and will heal their land. Now mine eyes shall be open, and mine ears attent unto the prayer that is made in this place." - 2 Chronicles 7:12-15

THE BATTLEFIELD OF INTERCESSORS

RESOURCE SECTION
THE 8 PRAYER WATCHES

THE BATTLEFIELD OF INTERCESSORS

THE FIRST (EVENING) WATCH

TIME: 6:00 p.m. – 9:00 p.m.

The Israelites ordered their prayer times accordingly, beginning with 6:00 p.m. – 9:00 p.m. which is a time of quiet reflection. Jesus used the evening watch to go aside and pray. (Matt. 14:15-23) In the early church, this watch at sundown was a time of corporate prayer (Vespers) where candles were lit, Psalms sung, thanksgiving offered, prayers said and blessings invoked. After the business of the day, it is a time to release anxieties to the Lord before sleep. During this watch, ask God to give you clear directions for the day ahead and about His call on your life.

THE SECOND WATCH

TIME: 9:00 p.m. – 12:00 a.m. (midnight)

Ps. 119:62 says, "At midnight I will rise to give thanks to You because of Your righteous judgments." It was at the midnight hour that God struck down the first-born of Egypt, and, consequently, His people were released from captivity and set free to worship Him. This watch is a time when God deals with the enemies that are trying to keep us from entering into His perfect plan for our lives. In the natural, this time is characterized by deep darkness. In the spiritual realm, the Second Watch is when diabolical assignments and sabotage are set in motion as supernatural creatures, including witches and demons and practices like black magic, collaborate to effect change and transformation for the evil one. It is important for intercessors at this watch to give thanks for the protection of the shadow of God's wing and pray for a visitation from the Lord. "Let God arise and His enemies be scattered."

THE THIRD WATCH

TIME: 12:00 a.m. – 3:00 a.m.

A period of much spiritual activity. It was the hour that caught Peter denying his Lord. Often we are awakened during this time with dreams God has given to us. God uses dreams and visions to bring instruction and counsel to us as we sleep and reveals areas where we need to concentrate our prayers and intercession. "In a dream, in a vision of the night, when deep sleep falls upon men, while slumbering on their beds, then He opens the ears of men, and seals their instructions." (Job 33:15) It is a time to pray to fortify yourself against doubt and unbelief and even the direction of your path. Be vigilant during this time and watch for God's revelation for breakthrough for His plans and purposes for your life and territory.

THE FOURTH WATCH

TIME: 3:00 a.m. – 6:00 a.m.

The spirit realm takes every word uttered from man as a command and mandate. Command your morning! Consecrate all the work for the day and pray for protection for God's people throughout the day. "You will make your prayer to Him, He will hear you, and you will pay your vows. You will also declare a thing and it will be established for you: so light will shine on your ways." (Job 22:27-28)

THE FIFTH WATCH

TIME: 6:00 a.m. – 9:00 a.m.

To watch is to set yourself to see what God will say to you. (Hab. 2:1) Practicing hearing the voice of God is essential to all the watches. One intercessor shared this insight, "I find the main focus of a watch is found this way: the Word and an event in time intersect. That's it! That is the target. It is like the scope on a gun. The point of the vertical Word and the horizontal time intersect (whether it is a sound, an event, a song). That point is the starting point of the watch."

THE SIXTH WATCH

TIME: 9:00 p.m. – 12:00 p.m. (noon)

It is generally accepted that this time period marked both Christ's sentencing by Pilate and crucifixion, and the descent of the Holy Spirit at Pentecost. The Israelites also observed this period as a time for corporate prayer. It was at this daily time of prayer and instruction at the temple that Peter and John were attending when they healed the lame man at the Gate Beautiful. (Acts 2: 1-8) The watchman guards and watches for the word of the Lord to be fulfilled. Pray for God's redemptive purposes in your life and region and watch how He answers your prayer during this time.

THE BATTLEFIELD OF INTERCESSORS

THE SEVENTH WATCH

TIME: 12:00 p.m. – 3:00 a.m.

Gives an hour of rest and a time to seek the Lord. Historically, we find Christ on the cross atoning for our sins. Redemption and restoration for mankind manifests through God's Son. Peter received the vision of the clean and unclean animals which heralded the inclusion of the Gentiles in God's redemptive plan. It was during this watch that Daniel always went home to pray and consequently was thrown into a den of lions. Daniel was delivered from the lions' den, and Daniel's accusers became the lions' dinner instead.

THE EIGHTH WATCH

TIME: 3:00 p.m. – 6:00 p.m.

Sees the close of the business day. It gives an opportunity for prayer. The Lord tells us to pray without ceasing. The Bible records a pattern and plan for daily prayer that marshals his army's forces. Beloved, it's time to watch and pray.

Prayer moves the hands of God. Even as He spoke the universe into creation, God created us in His image. Our spoken words and prayers carry the power of creation within them. As intercessors and God's watchmen on the walls of our families, cities and nations, we are called to watch over our assignments to see approaching danger and warn those endangered. (2Kings 9:17,18)

ABOUT THE AUTHOR
LORENA S. WOOTEN

Minister Lorena Wooten is the Author of "Fight for your Life" & Co-Founder of The Battlefield of Intercessors Prayer Ministry. Minister Lorena is a dedicated member of Agape Love Fellowship in Wilmington, DE where she leads prayer with fervency and power.

Please find her contact information, should you choose to reach her for invites and feedback: Lorenaswooten@gmail.com

Please follow her on Social Media @LorenaShakeraWooten.

To receive upcoming ministry newsletters and information, please join her email list Lorenaswooten@gmail.com.

To find out information about Intercessory Prayer Training, follow up on Facebook @TheBattlefieldofIntercessors or email: Lorenaswooten@gmail.com.

THE BATTLEFIELD OF INTERCESSORS